FEBRUARY ARTS AND CRAFTS

A MONTH OF ARTS AND CRAFTS AT YOUR FINGERTIPS!

Preschool–Kindergarten

Editors:
Mackie Rhodes
Jan Trautman

Artists:
Pam Crane
Theresa Lewis Goode
Rebecca Saunders

Cover Artist:
Kimberly Richard

www.themailbox.com

©2000 by THE EDUCATION CENTER, INC.
All rights reserved.
ISBN10 #1-56234-385-8 • ISBN13 #978-156234-385-9

Except as provided for herein, no part of this publication may be reproduced or transmitted in any form or by any means, electronic or mechanical, including photocopying, recording, or storing in any information storage and retrieval system or electronic online bulletin board, without prior written permission from The Education Center, Inc. Permission is given to the original purchaser to reproduce patterns and reproducibles for individual classroom use only and not for resale or distribution. Reproduction for an entire school or school system is prohibited. Please direct written inquiries to The Education Center, Inc., P.O. Box 9753, Greensboro, NC 27429-0753. The Education Center®, The Mailbox®, and the mailbox/post/grass logo are registered trademarks of The Education Center, Inc. All other brand or product names are trademarks or registered trademarks of their respective companies.

Manufactured in the United States

10 9 8 7 6 5 4 3

Table of Contents

Groundhog Garden 3
Groundhog Pop-Up Puppet 4
"Heart-y" Groundhog 5
Bubbly Toothbrush 6
Tooth Fairy Box 7
George Washington Hat 8
Holiday Hatchet 9
Lincoln Look-Alike Mask 10
Woven Heart Pocket 11
Bouquet of Love 12
Special Delivery 13
Candy Kiss 14
Valentine Box 15
Valentine Frog 16
Heart of My Kitchen 17
Valentine Puzzle 18
Lovely Suncatcher 19
Flap Jack 20
Spell It With Pancakes! 21
Paper Plate Orca 22
Wonderful Whales 23
Patterns 24

Groundhog Garden

Is spring just around the corner or will winter linger on? These groundhog planters will help your little ones forecast the weather and start their spring planting, too!

Materials (per child)

- 2½" brown craft foam circle
- two ¾" brown pom-poms (ears)
- two 1" brown pom-poms (paws)
- 1 black mini pom-pom (nose)
- 2 wiggle eyes
- 1 spring-type clothespin
- red craft foam
- 8-oz. foam cup
- soil
- seeds
- pencil
- crayons
- black permanent marker
- scissors
- craft glue

Directions

1. To make a groundhog, glue the wiggle eyes and black nose onto the foam circle.
2. Cut out a red foam mouth; then glue it onto the groundhog.
3. To make ears and paws, glue the pom-poms onto the groundhog as shown.
4. On one side of the cup, use the black marker to draw a groundhog shadow. Write "More Winter" near the shadow.
5. Use crayons to draw flowers on the opposite side of the cup. Write "Early Spring" near the flowers.
6. Fill the planter with soil; then plant a few seeds in the soil.
7. Glue the groundhog to a clothespin. After the glue dries, clip the clothespin to the planter.

Julie Koczur—VAFB, CA

Teacher Tips

- If desired, substitute construction paper for the craft foam.
- Plant seeds that have a short germination period, such as grass or marigolds.
- On Groundhog Day, set the planter outdoors to see whether or not it casts a shadow. Attach the groundhog to the corresponding side.

Groundhog Pop-Up Puppet

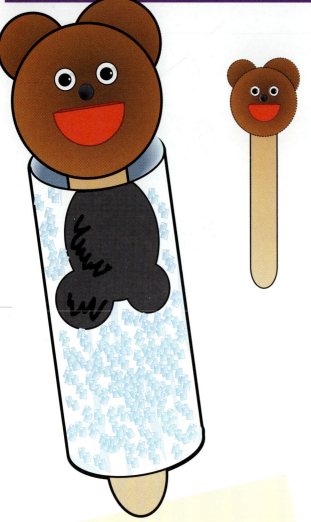

These fuzzy groundhogs will be popping up everywhere to predict whether or not the end of winter is near. Invite your little ones to take these cute critters outdoors on Groundhog Day to make their own forecasts for the season.

Materials (per child)

- 1 toilet paper tube
- 1 wide craft stick
- 1 large (1 1/2") brown pom-pom
- 2 small brown pom-poms (ears)
- 2 wiggle eyes
- 1 small black craft foam nose
- 1 red craft foam mouth
- white glue paint (see Teacher Tips)
- clear glitter
- black permanent marker
- craft glue
- paintbrush

Directions

1. Glue the large pom-pom to one end of the craft stick.
2. Glue on two pom-pom ears, the wiggle eyes, the black nose, and the red mouth.
3. To make a winter hole for the groundhog, paint the tube with the glue paint. Sprinkle glitter on the wet paint.
4. When the paint is dry, use the marker to draw a groundhog shadow on the tube, as shown.
5. Gently insert the puppet into the winter hole. To make the groundhog pop up, simply use the handle to push the puppet out of the hole.

Teacher Tips

- To make white glue paint, mix equal amounts of white tempera paint and glue.
- Have each child rotate the puppet in the hole so that sometimes it sees its shadow when it pops out, and at other times it only sees the snowy ground.

Julie Koczur—VAFB, CA

"Heart-y" Groundhog

There's one thing for sure—this little guy's got a lot of heart! Display these lovable critters on a bulletin board to greet the month of February.

Materials (per child)

- tagboard heart tracers (see Teacher Tips)
- small white construction paper heart, for teeth (page 24)
- construction paper eyes (page 25)
- 1 large sheet of brown construction paper
- black construction paper
- flat, plain-colored toothpicks
- markers
- scissors
- glue

Step 2

Directions

1. Fold the brown construction paper in half. Place the straight edge of the large heart tracer on the fold; then trace it and cut it out. *Do not cut on the fold.*
2. To make ears, trace the smaller heart tracer on brown paper. Cut out the heart; then cut it in half (each half will be an ear).
3. Cut out a black construction paper nose. Then cut out the eyes and the small white heart (for teeth).
4. Glue the ears, eyes, nose, and teeth onto the large heart as shown. Then glue on toothpick whiskers.
5. Use markers to add details to the groundhog.

Teacher Tips

- To make tracers, cut out tagboard copies of the large half heart pattern and the smaller heart pattern on page 24.
- If desired, glue a wide craft stick to the groundhog to make a puppet.
- To convert this project into a mask, cut out eyeholes instead of gluing eyes on the face. Then add a wide craft stick handle.

Margaret Southard—Cleveland, NY

Bubbly Toothbrush

Make toothbrushing a bubbly occasion with these special toothbrushes. To promote dental hygiene, encourage each child to display her picture at home as a reminder to brush long enough to make lots of fun toothpaste bubbles.

(Note: Balloons can be a choking hazard for small children. Please supervise children closely during this activity.)

Materials (per child)

- construction paper toothbrush (page 25)
- 1 sheet of dark construction paper
- tray of white tempera paint
- 1 small balloon (softly inflated)
- toilet paper tube
- glue
- scissors

Directions

1. Cut out the toothbrush; then glue it onto the construction paper.
2. Dip the balloon in the paint. Use a light bouncing motion to balloon-paint on and around the toothbrush bristles.
3. To give the appearance of bubbles, use the end of the tube to randomly print white circles on the balloon prints.

Teacher Tips
- Inflate the balloons for this activity in advance.
- If desired, invite the child to mix the color of her preferred toothpaste by adding a drop of blue, green, or red paint to a personal portion of white paint.

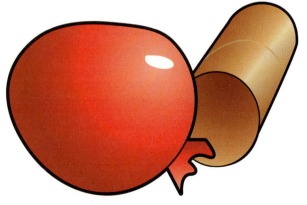

Margaret Southard—Cleveland, NY

Tooth Fairy Box

Invite each child to create this sparkling tooth box to take home. Encourage him to use the box to safely hold his little white gems as he awaits the tooth fairy's visit.

Materials (per child)

- white construction paper tooth pattern (page 27)
- text cloud (page 27)
- 1 individual-size milk carton
- white glue paint (see Teacher Tips)
- 1 paper fastener
- 5" length of pipe cleaner
- glitter
- scissors
- paintbrush
- clear tape
- hole puncher
- glue

Directions

1. Pull open all sides of the milk carton top. Cut off three sides of the top, leaving one side to use as a fold-down lid (as shown).
2. Paint the outside of the carton with white glue paint; then sprinkle glitter on the wet paint. Let it dry.
3. Cut out the tooth pattern and text cloud. Fold the tooth cutout in half and at both ends where indicated. Glue the folded ends together to make a stand-up figure (as shown).
4. Punch a hole one-half inch from the top of the box front. Secure the paper fastener in the hole; then tape the fastener ends in place.
5. Make a pipe cleaner loop. Poke the ends of the loop into the box lid. To secure the loop, spread the ends out and tape them in place.
6. Glue the stand-up tooth on the box lid.
7. Glue the text cloud on the front. Let the glue dry.
8. To use, put a lost tooth in the box. Close the lid and hook the loop over the fastener.

Teacher Tips

- To make glue paint, mix equal amounts of white paint and glue.
- If necessary, poke a pushpin in the lid to start the hole for the pipe cleaner loop.
- Use a large paper clip to hold the tooth in place on the lid while the glue dries.

Sue DeRiso—Barrington, RI

George Washington Hat

To celebrate Presidents' Day, invite each child to make and proudly wear this patriotic, three-cornered hat. What a perfect prop for a parade or for dramatic-play activities.

Materials (per child)

- 1 construction paper hat pattern in each color: red, white, blue (page 26)
- 1 yellow construction paper medallion (page 26)
- red craft feather
- scissors
- glue
- stapler

Step 2

Directions

1. Cut out the medallion and each hat pattern.
2. Poke the end of the feather through the blue hat pattern as shown.
3. Glue the medallion over the feather and let the glue dry.
4. Staple one end of the blue hat to one end of the red hat. Then staple the other end of the blue hat to the white hat.
5. Staple the loose ends of the white and red hats together.

Teacher Tips

- If needed, use a pushpin to start the holes in the blue hat; then insert the feather.
- As you staple the ends together, adjust the hat to fit the child's head.

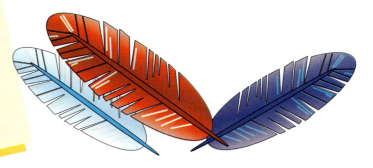

Susan Bunyan—Dodge City, KS

Holiday Hatchet

Share the story of George Washington and the cherry tree; then have each child make this Presidents' Day commemorative hatchet. Invite students to use their hatchets as they role-play young George in the story.

Materials (per child)

- gray construction paper hatchet head (page 25)
- green construction paper leaves (page 25)
- 1 sheet of brown construction paper
- 2 red pom-poms
- 4" length of green yarn
- small stapler
- glue
- scissors

Directions

1. Cut out the hatchet head and leaf patterns.
2. To make a hatchet handle, roll the brown paper into a tube and staple the ends.
3. Cut a three-inch slit in one end of the handle; then cut another three-inch slit opposite the first one.
4. Slide the hatchet head into the slits on the handle. Staple the head in place through all thicknesses.
5. To make cherries, glue a pom-pom to each end of the yarn and let the glue dry.
6. Staple the string of cherries to the hatchet as shown. Then glue the leaves on top of the cherry stems.

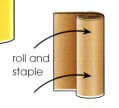

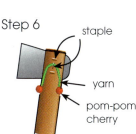

Teacher Tip

● Glue the edge of the brown paper to the tube along the section that is not reachable with the stapler. This will secure the edge more firmly.

Susan Bunyan—Dodge City, KS

Lincoln Look-Alike Mask

Enhance your Presidents' Day unit with these Abraham Lincoln masks. During group time, invite each child to don her mask as she shares a Lincoln fact with the class.

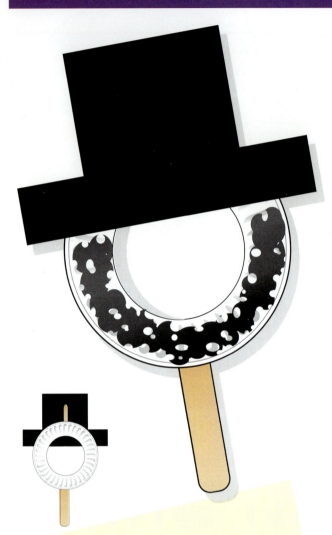

Materials (per child)

- one 9" paper plate
- 1 sheet of black construction paper
- 1 wide craft stick
- cotton balls
- black tempera paint
- scissors
- glue

Directions

1. Cut out the center of the paper plate, creating a ring from the plate rim.
2. Use cotton balls to dab black paint around the rim. Let the paint dry.
3. Fold the black paper in half; then cut out a stovepipe hat shape as shown.
4. Glue the hat to the top of the painted ring.
5. Glue a craft stick handle to the back of the ring (beard).

Teacher Tips

- Use a clothespin to hold the handle in place while the glue dries.
- If necessary, to reinforce the hat so that it stands up, slide a regular craft stick between the plate rim and the hat; then glue it in place.

Sue DeRiso—Barrington, RI

Woven Heart Pocket

Little fingers weave lots of love into this special heart pocket. Invite each child to use his pocket to collect valentines. Or have him fill it with an edible treat to give to a loved one.

Materials (per child)

- large tagboard heart tracers (see Teacher Tips)
- white poster board
- red poster board
- seasonal ribbons
- scissors
- decorative edging scissors
- glue
- pencil

Directions

1. Trace the larger heart onto white poster board. Cut it out with decorative scissors.
2. Trace the smaller heart onto red poster board; then cut it out.
3. Fold the red heart in half. Cut slits in the heart as shown, spacing them one-half inch apart.
4. Unfold the heart and then weave lengths of ribbon through the slits in an alternating pattern. Trim the excess ribbon.
5. Glue the edges of the red heart to the white heart, leaving the top open to create a pocket.

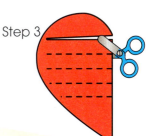
Step 3

Teacher Tips

- To make tracers, cut out two tagboard hearts, one slightly smaller than the other. If desired, use the large heart pattern on page 24 as a guide for the tracers.

- If desired, add a ribbon loop to the back of the pocket for display purposes.

Julie Koczur—VAFB, CA

Bouquet of Love

This vase full of happy hearts and beautiful blooms is the perfect gift for each child to present to a special loved one.

Materials (per child)

- tagboard heart and flower tracers (see Teacher Tips)
- 1 laundry detergent bottle lid
- pipe cleaners (cut about 1" longer than the lid height)
- Styrofoam® block cut to fit inside lid
- pink, white, and red foam trays
- pencil with blunt point (or ballpoint pen)
- seasonal or red ribbon
- heart confetti or punch-outs
- scissors
- craft glue

Directions

1. To make a vase, decorate the lid with the ribbon and heart confetti.
2. Trace several hearts and/or flowers on the foam trays; then cut out each shape.
3. Gently poke one end of a pipe cleaner into each cutout.
4. Poke the free end of each pipe cleaner into the foam block.
5. Press the foam block firmly into the bottom of the vase.
6. Spread out, bend, and turn the hearts and/or blooms to arrange them as desired.

Teacher Tips

- To make tracers, draw a few different heart and flower sizes onto tagboard; then cut them out. If desired, copy a few different sizes of the small heart pattern (page 24) onto tagboard; then cut them out.
- If desired, invite children to embellish the hearts and blooms with glitter, sequins, and seasonal confetti before putting them in the foam block.

Margaret Southard—Cleveland, NY

Special Delivery

Invite each child to arrange this lovely bouquet and then deliver it to someone special on Valentine's Day.

Materials (per child)

- tagboard heart tracers (see Teacher Tips)
- red, pink, white, and green construction paper
- 1/4 sheet of red, pink, or white tissue paper
- ribbon in seasonal colors
- scissors
- glue
- stapler
- pencil

Directions

1. Trace several hearts on your choice of paper colors and cut them out.
2. Cut a 4 1/2-inch green paper stem for each heart. Glue a heart onto each stem; then let the glue dry.
3. Arrange the hearts into a bouquet. Staple the stems together at the bottom.
4. Wrap the tissue paper around the bouquet and tie a ribbon around it.

Teacher Tips

- To make tracers, cut out a few different tagboard heart sizes. Or cut out tagboard copies of the heart pattern (page 24) to use as tracers.
- If desired, have the child decorate the hearts with glitter crayons or glitter.

Kimberli Carrier—Nashua, NH

Candy Kiss

This giant candy kiss will get your youngsters in the mood for the real thing! So surprise each child with a real candy kiss after she completes this project!

Materials (per child)

tagboard candy kiss tracer (see Teacher Tips)
white construction paper
1 sheet of tagboard
12" square of aluminum foil
permanent markers
scissors
glue
tape

Directions

1. Fold the sheet of tagboard in half. Place the straight edge of the tracer on the fold; then trace it and cut it out. *Do not cut on the fold.*
2. Unfold the kiss cutout. Then gently wrap the foil shiny side up around the kiss. Glue the edges of the foil to the back.
3. Cut out a ribbon shape from white construction paper. Tape the ribbon to the back of the kiss.
4. Use markers to write your name on the ribbon and to draw a face on the candy.

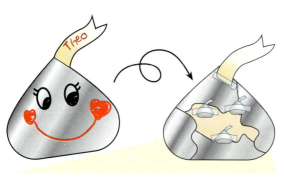

Teacher Tips
- To make a tracer, cut out a tagboard copy of the candy kiss pattern on page 27.
- Tape a few candies to the back of the child's candy kiss as a special valentine surprise.

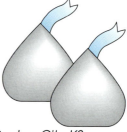

Susan Bunyan—Dodge City, KS

14

Valentine Box

This pretty valentine box is durable and easy to use. Have youngsters drop their valentines in the corresponding boxes. Then, during your valentine celebration, invite each child to open the flap on his box to retrieve his special messages.

Materials (per child)

- 1 covered cube-shaped tissue box (see Teacher Tips)
- tempera paint (to match or complement the covered box color)
- seasonal confetti, stickers, and assorted heart cutouts
- 2 1/2" length of pipe cleaner
- craft knife (for teacher use)
- paintbrush
- scissors
- permanent marker
- craft glue
- hole puncher

Directions

1. Paint the top of the tissue box. Let the paint dry.
2. Use the marker to write your name on the flap.
3. Decorate the box with valentine confetti, stickers, and heart cutouts.
4. Punch a hole in the box top and another in the flap as shown.
5. Thread one end of the pipe cleaner through the hole in the flap; then twist it to secure it.
6. Shape the other end of the pipe cleaner into a hook. Insert it into the hole in the box top.
7. To use, deposit valentine cards (and small treats) in the top opening of the box. Then unhook and open the flap to remove the goodies.

Ada Goren—Winston Salem, NC

Teacher Tip

- In advance, cover the sides of the box with a 5 1/2" x 18" piece of red, pink, or white Con-Tact® covering. Use the craft knife to cut along the edges as shown. Then cut out a heart-shaped flap with scissors.

Valentine Frog

This cute little green guy is sure to leap out as a valentine favorite! Display each child's "heart-y" frog in your classroom; then have her deliver it to a loved one on Valentine's Day.

Hop to it... be my valentine!

Materials (per child)

tagboard heart and circle tracers (see Teacher Tips)
1 large sheet of dark green construction paper
1 sheet of light green construction paper
1 construction paper basket (page 28)
1 pair of light green construction paper arms (page 29)
2 small light green construction paper hearts (page 24)
1 pair of white construction paper frog eyes (page 30)
scissors
glue
black marker

Directions

1. Fold the dark green paper in half. Place the straight edge of the heart tracer on the fold; then trace it and cut it out. *Do not cut on the fold.*
2. Outline the circle tracer twice onto light green paper. Cut out the circles; then fringe-cut each one to create eyelashes.
3. Cut out the eyes, cheeks (small hearts), arms, and basket patterns.
4. Glue the eyes onto the large heart. Glue an eyelid with lashes onto each eye.
5. Glue on the light green cheeks, then draw a mouth on the frog.
6. Glue each arm to the frog where indicated.
7. Loop one arm through the basket handle; then glue that hand to the frog. Also glue the other hand to the frog.

Teacher Tips
- To make the heart tracer, cut out a tagboard copy of the large heart pattern on page 24. Cut out a tagboard copy of a frog eye pattern (page 30) to use as a circle tracer.
- To curl the eyelashes, wrap them around a pencil and then release them.

Susan Bunyan—Dodge City, KS

Heart of My Kitchen

Tuck a note into this unique message holder to explain its purpose—that is, to provide a special place for family members to leave heartfelt messages for each other. Then encourage each child to display his holder on a magnetic surface in his kitchen.

Materials (per child)

- two 9" paper plates
- red, pink, and purple tissue paper hearts in assorted sizes
- paper punch hearts
- 12" length of red ribbon
- scissors
- glue
- hole puncher
- magnetic tape
- paintbrush
- water-diluted glue

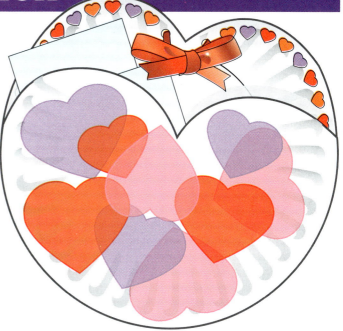

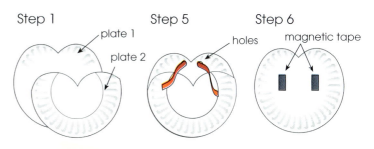

Directions

1. Trim the edge of one paper plate to look like the top of a heart. Repeat with the second plate, but trim it so that it is shorter than the first one (see illustration).
2. Glue tissue paper hearts all over the back of the smaller plate. Then paint a coat of water-diluted glue over the hearts. Let the glue dry.
3. Glue a border of paper punch hearts on the heart-shaped edge of the large plate.
4. With the decorated side facing out, glue the small plate to the large plate along the uncut rims.
5. After the glue dries, punch two holes in the large plate as shown. Lace a ribbon through the holes; then tie it into a bow.
6. Attach two magnetic tape strips to the back of the holder.

adapted from ideas by Julie Koczur—VAFB, CA
Sue DeRiso—Barrington, RI

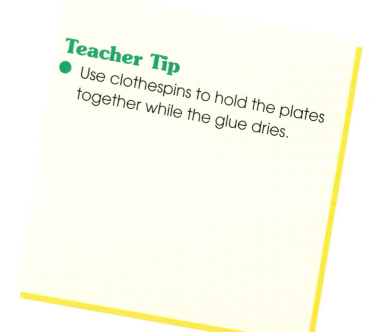

Teacher Tip
- Use clothespins to hold the plates together while the glue dries.

Valentine Puzzle

This bundle of sticks holds a clever little surprise—a valentine puzzle! Ask each child to challenge a friend to assemble her sticks to discover the special valentine greeting.

Materials (per child)

- 6 wide craft sticks
- markers
- masking tape
- red or pink ribbon

Directions

1. Tape the craft sticks together to create a panel as shown.
2. Turn the panel over. Use markers to draw a valentine picture and/or write a special message on the panel.
3. Remove the tape from the back of the panel to separate the sticks.
4. Stack the sticks in random order; then tie a ribbon around them.
5. To use, unwrap the sticks; then put them together to display the picture and/or greeting.

Teacher Tip
- As an alternative to tying the sticks together with ribbon, invite the child to decorate a white envelope; then have her put the sticks in it.

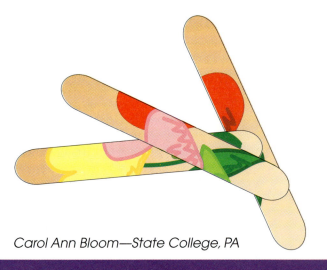

Carol Ann Bloom—State College, PA

Lovely Suncatcher

Warm up your classroom with these lovely creations! Throughout February, display the suncatchers in your classroom window to capture the beauty of the winter sun.

Materials (per child)

- tagboard heart tracer (see Teacher Tips)
- 2 large sheets of red construction paper
- 12" x 15" piece of clear Con-Tact® covering
- tissue paper hearts in assorted colors and sizes (see Teacher Tips)
- clear glitter
- pencil
- scissors
- craft glue

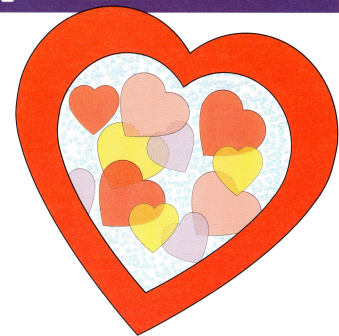

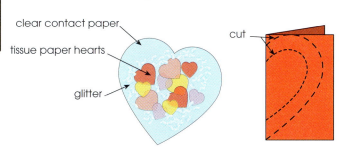

clear contact paper
tissue paper hearts
glitter
cut

Directions

1. To make heart rings, fold each sheet of red construction paper in half. Place the straight edge of the heart tracer on the fold of each sheet; then trace the outer and inner edges of it. Cut out the shape on both lines. *Do not cut on the fold.*
2. Fold the Con-Tact covering in half. Place the straight edge of the heart tracer on the fold. Trace *only* the outer edge of the tracer with a pencil; then cut out the shape.
3. Remove the backing from the Con-Tact covering. Randomly place tissue paper hearts on the sticky side of the covering.
4. Sprinkle glitter onto the remaining sticky areas of the covering.
5. Glue the decorated covering between the two heart rings.

Teacher Tips

- To make a heart tracer, cut out a tagboard copy of the large heart pattern (page 24). Then, starting and ending on the straight edge, cut 1 1/2 inches inside the curve of the shape. (Use this tracer for the heart rings in Step 1 and the heart in Step 2.)
- If desired, enlarge and reduce the small heart pattern on page 24; then use the different heart sizes as guides to cut out tissue paper hearts.

Julie Koczur—VAFB, CA

Flap Jack

This pancake chef puppet will have youngsters' mouths watering for the real thing.

Materials (per child)

- tagboard circle tracer (see Teacher Tip)
- white construction paper eyes, apron, hat, and hand (pages 30–31)
- red construction paper mouth and mitt (pages 30–31)
- tagboard spatula (page 30)
- 1 brown paper lunch bag
- two 1½" x 3" tagboard strips
- yellow construction paper
- aluminum foil
- crayons
- brown and white tempera paint
- sponge
- cotton swab
- permanent marker
- scissors
- glue

Directions

1. Outline the circle tracer on yellow paper. Cut it out and sponge-paint it light brown.
2. Cut out all of the patterns. Use the cotton swab and white paint to decorate the mitt and to make the mouth resemble a bacon strip. Let the paint dry.
3. Color the center of each eye yellow. Decorate the apron as desired.
4. Glue the mouth and eyes on the circle. Cover the spatula with foil, gluing the edges to the back. Draw slots on the spatula with the marker.
5. Glue the mitt on the end of a tagboard strip. Glue the hand and spatula on the other strip.
6. Glue the head, hat, arms, and apron onto the bag as shown.

Sue DeRiso—Barrington, RI

Teacher Tip

- To make a circle tracer, cut out a 5-inch tagboard circle.

Spell It With Pancakes!

Fill youngsters' plates with these pancakes to promote letter, name, and word recognition. Ask each child to "read" his plate to the class; then display all of the plates to reinforce the letters and words represented on them.

Materials (per child)

3 1/2" tagboard circle tracer
paper plate (any solid color)
plastic fork
white paper
2" die-cut letters
brown crayon
scissors
glue

Directions

1. Trace a circle on white paper for each letter to be used. Then cut out each circle (pancake).
2. Place each pancake over the desired letter. Rub a brown crayon over it until the letter appears.
3. Sequence the pancakes to spell the desired word. Then glue them onto the plate.
4. Glue the fork to the plate.

Teacher Tips

- For best results, limit the number of letters to five per plate.
- Arrange the letters in horizontal, vertical, or diagonal rows or around the plate rim.
- To give the pancakes a buttery look, paint a yellow watercolor wash on each one.

Margaret Southard—Cleveland, NY

Paper Plate Orca

Try this whale of an idea to add interest and fun to your whales unit. Then display these awesome orcas on an underwater background.

Materials (per child)

tagboard fin, flipper, and belly tracers (see Teacher Tips)
three 6" paper plates
black construction paper
red construction paper scraps
2 small black beads (or pom-poms)
white chalk
black tempera paint
paintbrush
scissors
glue
pencil

Directions

1. Paint the bottom of one paper plate black and let it dry.
2. With the insides facing together, glue the rim of the painted plate to the second plate to make the whale's body. (The front is black and the back is white.)
3. Fit the belly to the curve of the third plate. Trace and cut out the belly.
4. Cut out a red paper wedge to fit the inside curve of the belly. Glue the wedge in place to serve as a mouth.
5. Use chalk to outline the fin and flipper tracers on black paper. Cut out each shape.
6. Glue the fin and flipper to the back of the whale. Then glue the belly and two black bead eyes to the front of the whale.

Margaret Southard—Cleveland, NY

Teacher Tips

- To make tracers, cut out a tagboard copy of the fin, flipper, and belly patterns on page 32.
- Use clothespins to hold the plates together while the glue dries.

Wonderful Whales

Your little ones will have a lot to spout about when they create these models of whales. Invite each child to show off her whale as she shares her knowledge of this fascinating mammal with the class.

Materials (per child)

- construction paper flipper (page 32)
- construction paper spout (page 32)
- construction paper scraps
- 1 small paper bag
- two 1" wiggle eyes
- newspaper scraps
- tempera paint (in any whale color)
- paintbrush
- scissors
- masking tape
- clear tape
- glue

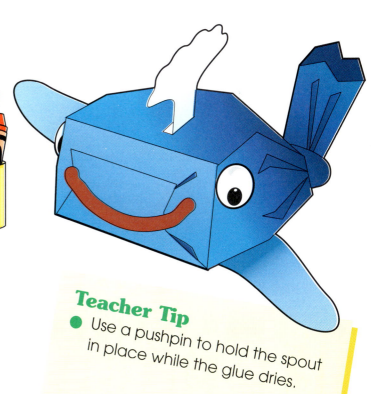

Directions

1. Half-fill the bag with newspaper scraps. Twist the middle of the bag to close it; then wrap masking tape around the twisted section.
2. Paint the bag. Allow the paint to dry.
3. Cut out the flipper and spout patterns. Also cut out a mouth shape. Fold the spout where indicated.
4. Glue the wiggle eyes, mouth, and spout onto the bag as shown.
5. Cut the flipper in half. Glue half a flipper to each side of the whale, using clear tape to hold each one in place.

Teacher Tip
- Use a pushpin to hold the spout in place while the glue dries.

Sue DeRiso—Barrington, RI

Heart Patterns
Use with " 'Heart-y' Groundhog" on page 5, "Valentine Frog" on page 16, and "Lovely Suncatcher" on page 19.

Place on fold.

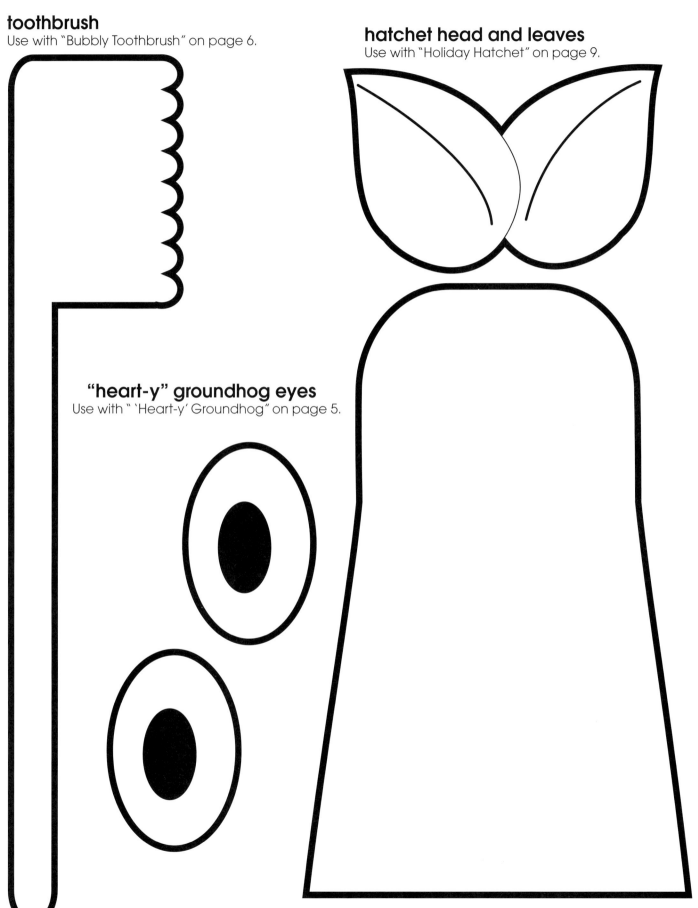

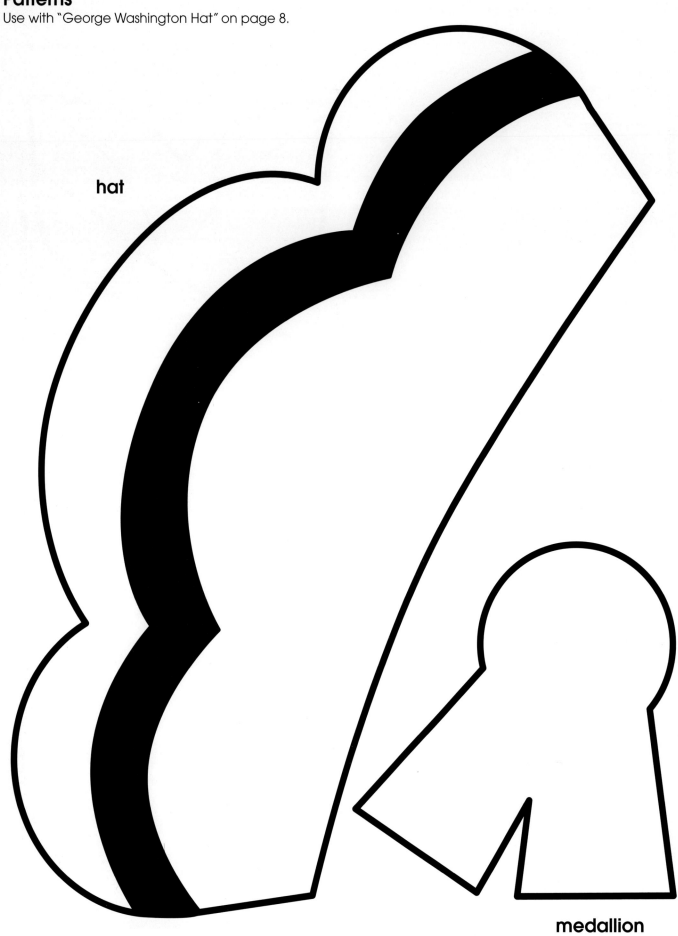

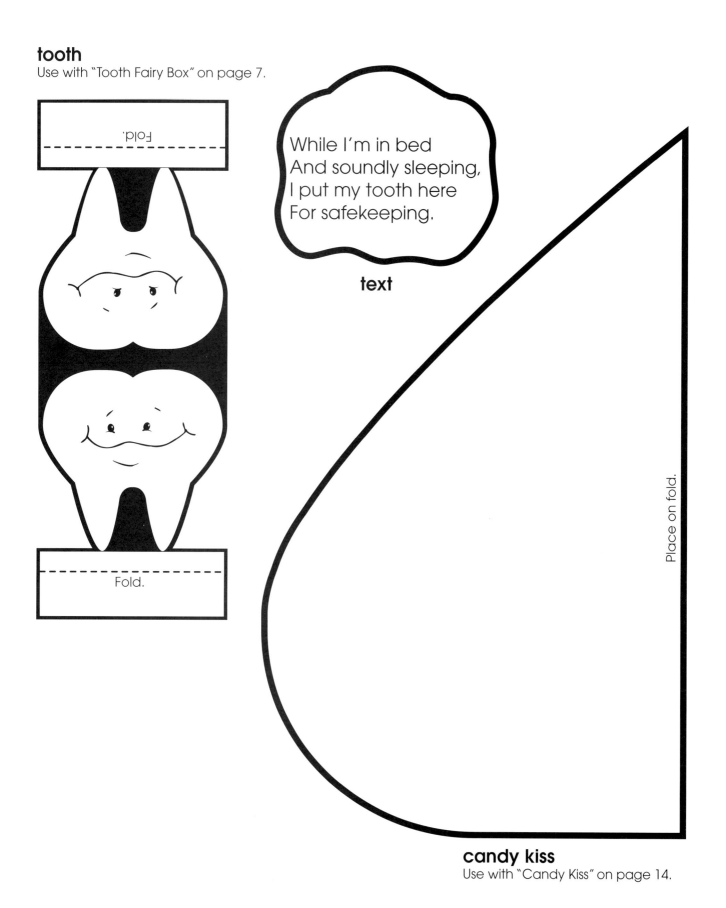

Basket Pattern
Use with "Valentine Frog" on page 16.

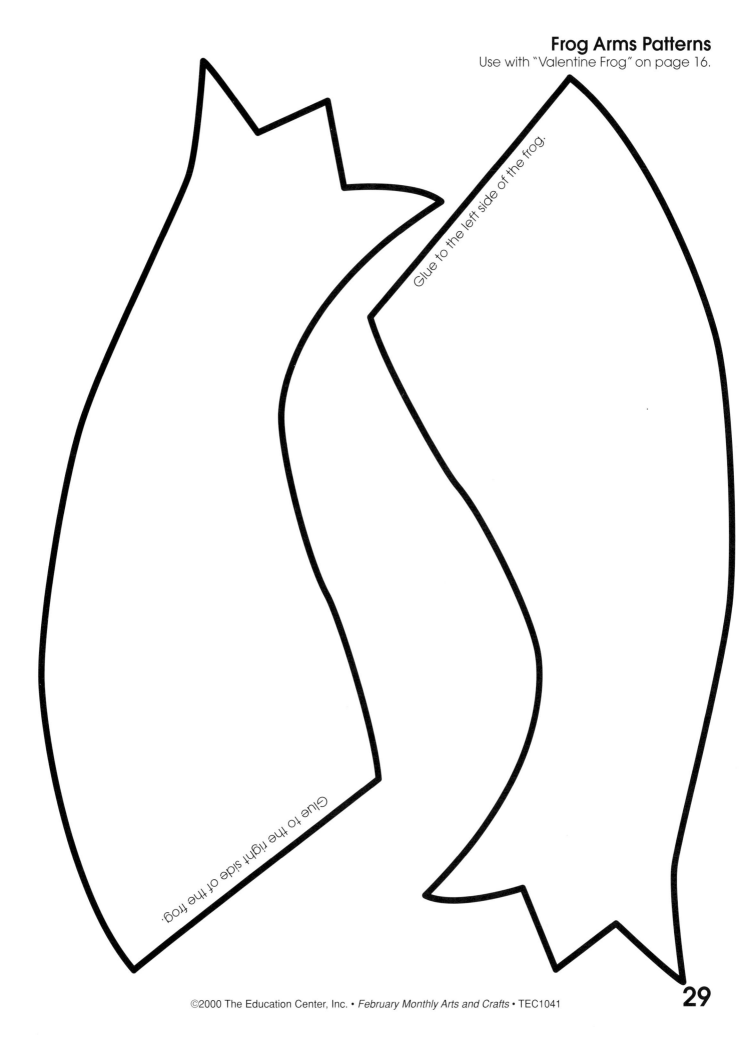

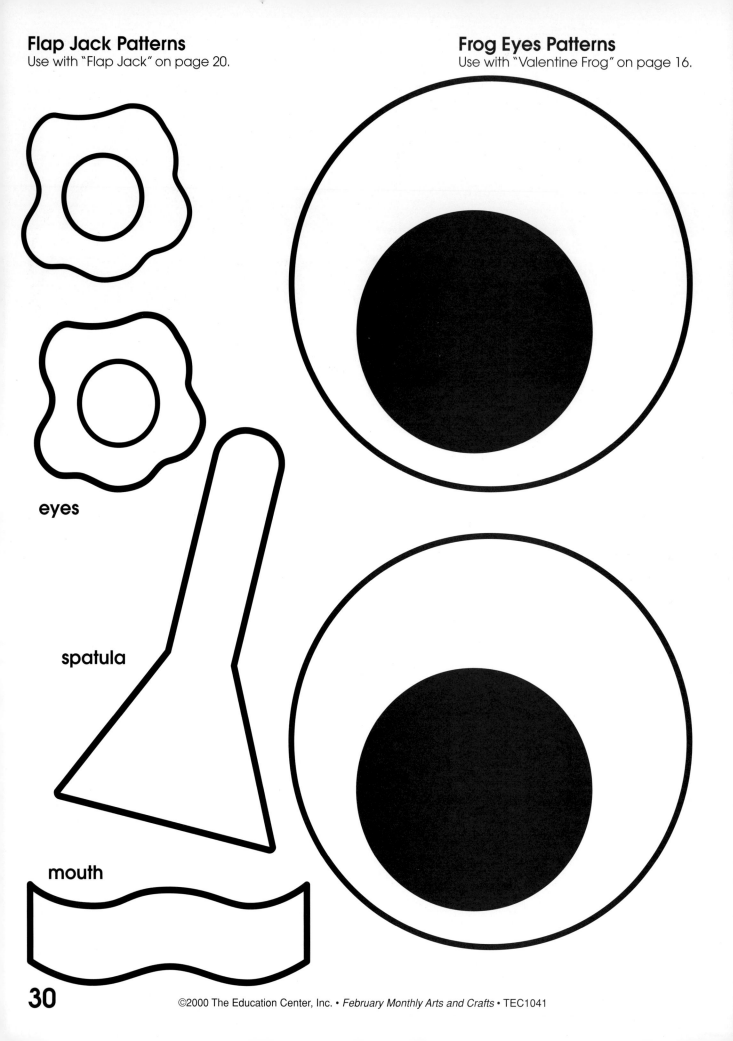

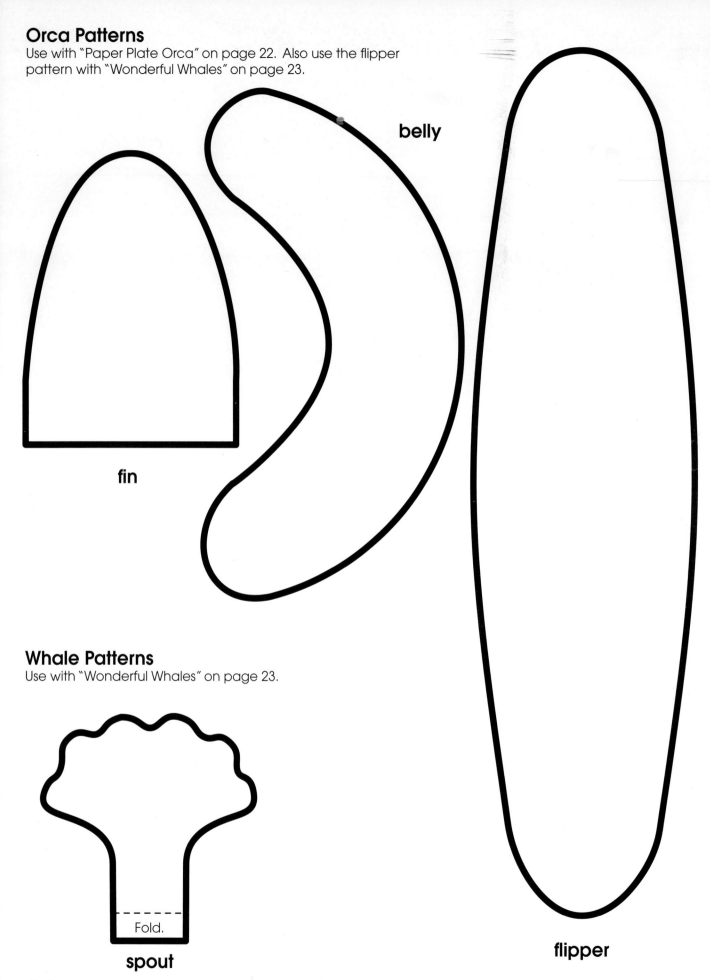